Covenants Old and New

W M Henry

ISBN: 978-1-78364-448-3

The Open Bible Trust
Fordland Mount, Upper Basildon,
Reading, RG8 8LU, UK.

www.obt.org.uk

Covenants:

Old and New

Contents

Introduction

Introduction

The Christian Bible is divided into two parts – the Old Testament and the New Testament. The word "testament" is usually translated "covenant" in the Scriptures and this word is significant in connection with God's relationship with His people.

A covenant is an agreement between two parties, whereby each agrees to observe certain conditions. Streets says:

> In the Scriptures a covenant is a singularly solemn and binding contract or agreement between man and man, or between God and man, the terms of which were attested and ratified by sacrifice. (Ernest Streets, *Think on These Things:* p103; chapter on *The Covenants*)

The last point is important.

> The sacrifice used in confirmation of a stated covenant was cut, divided and set out in a particular manner , and the parties to the agreement then being entered into observed a special ritual of passing or walking through or between the pieces or parts so cut, divided and set out before them ... In this way... they bound themselves to keep and observe the conditions of the agreement then made, by putting themselves, as it were, into the sacrifice and becoming part of it, and, as they walked between the cut pieces, saying, in effect ... "May I thus be cut, divided and destroyed if I fail to keep the promise now made." (*ibid*, p103)

This feature is prominent in Jeremiah 34:18, where we read of the Lord's warning to Judah that He will punish them for breaking His covenant:

> "The men who have violated my covenant and have not fulfilled the terms of the covenant they made before me, I will treat like the calf they cut in two and then walked between its pieces."

Covenant in the Scriptures

Covenant in the Scriptures

In the Old Testament, "covenant" is the Hebrew word *beriyth*. It occurs many times and is occasionally rendered "allies" or "treaty" (always with reference to confederacies between different kingdoms). The word is used in relation to a covenant between God and man in the Old Testament in relation to four individuals – Noah, Abraham, Moses and David.

In addition, Jeremiah 31 foresees a new covenant between the Lord and the re-united houses of Israel and this prophecy is picked up and developed by the New Testament writers in relation to the Lord Jesus Christ.

In the NIV New Testament "covenant" is the Greek word *diatheke*, which sometimes appears in the KJV as "testament" (e.g. 1 Corinthians 11:25).

However, although the word appears in 11 of the 27 New Testament books, the references are few and far between. Excluding the epistle to the Hebrews (where the word is used 17 times), it occurs only 16 times in the New Testament. These references can be subdivided as follows:

Covenant	Gospels	Acts	Paul's writings during Acts	Paul's writings post Acts	Revelation
The Lord's mention of the new covenant at the last supper	Matt. 26:28 Mark 14:24 Luke 22:20		1Cor.11:25		
God's covenant with Abraham in the Old Testament	Luke 1:72	Acts 3:25 Acts 7:8	Gal. 3:17		
Paul and others as ministers of the new covenant			2 Cor. 3:6		
Prediction of the coming new covenant			Rom. 11:27		
Reference to the Jewish Scriptures as the "old covenant"			2 Cor. 3:14		
Reference to covenants with Hagar and Sarah			Gal. 4:24		

Statement that the covenants belong to Israel			Rom. 9:4		
Historic description of Gentiles as aliens to the covenants				Eph. 2:12	
Vision of the ark of the covenant in heaven					Rev. 11:19
Human covenants for trading purposes			Gal. 3:15		

God's covenant with Noah was His first covenant with humanity. It was an unconditional covenant with all mankind – indeed, with all creatures on the earth, never to destroy the world again in a flood. The sign of the rainbow is a token of that promise.

The covenants made with Abraham, Moses and David are connected with one another. The Abrahamic covenant was with Abraham and his descendants and was confirmed to his son Isaac and grandson Jacob (Israel). It emphasised their growth as a nation, promising them a land of their own. The Mosaic covenant was given to the children of Israel and made known God's purposes for them in greater depth, as they prepared to *enter* that land. The Davidic covenant concerned David and his descendants, concerning their kingship over the people of Israel *in* the land. But the most awesome fact is that these three covenants all find their consummation in the new covenant and in the person of the Lord Jesus Christ.

This booklet therefore focuses on the three covenants made with these great men of the Old Testament and the ways in which they come together in the new covenant and in the work of Christ. It will also consider the extent to which these truths impact upon the situation of the Christian church in the twenty-first century.

The Lord's Covenant with Abraham

The Lord's Covenant with Abraham

An unconditional promise

In Genesis 12:1-3, we read of God's call to Abram to leave his country and people and go to a new land. Abram was given a fourfold promise in these verses:

- He was going to be a great nation.
- He would be given a land.
- He would be blessed.
- All peoples of the earth would be blessed through him.

This promise about his offspring and the land was repeated in Genesis 13 after Lot had separated from Abram.

At the start of chapter 15, Abram spoke to God when He appeared to him in a vision and addressed Him as "Sovereign Lord" (Genesis 15:2). In this vision God confirmed to Abram that he would have a son from his own body and that his offspring would be like the stars in the sky. Secondly, the Lord promised him that he and his descendants would be given the land, which is identified in 15:18 as being the area between the river of Egypt and the Euphrates.

In Genesis 15:8 Abram asked the Lord for a sign that he would indeed take possession of this land:

> But Abram said, "O Sovereign Lord, how can I know that I will gain possession of it?"

The Lord's response was to set the scene for a covenant to be made (confirmed in verse 18). Abram was instructed to bring a series of animals and birds for the offering of the covenant, and, as was the custom, divided the carcases into two halves and set them opposite one another (verse 10).

As suggested on page 3, the next stage in the process should have been for both parties to the covenant to pass between the pieces of meat in order to demonstrate their commitment to the conditions of the agreement.

However, what actually happened was rather more curious. In Genesis 15:12 we read that Abram fell into a deep sleep and a thick and dreadful darkness came over him. In his nightmare the Lord foretold the suffering of his descendants in Egypt and their ultimate deliverance four hundred years later[1].

But in verses 17-18 we read:

> When the sun had set and darkness had fallen, a smoking firepot with a blazing torch appeared and passed between the pieces. On that day the Lord made a covenant with Abram and said, "To your descendants I give this land, from the river of Egypt to the great river, the Euphrates ..."

It is not clear whether Abram was still asleep but it is significant that the Lord alone passed between the pieces; Abram was not invited to join Him because the covenant that was being made was

---

[1] In Exodus 12:40-41 we read that the Israelites lived in Egypt for 430 years "to the very day." Presumably the additional 30 years refers to the time before the Pharaoh who "did not know about Joseph" (Exodus 1:8) came to power. During this time the Israelites were not oppressed.

an *unconditional*, one-way covenant. It was more of a promise than an agreement, which ensured the certainty that it will be fulfilled, although exactly when is unclear.

This is the first mention of a covenant with Abram and this covenant relationship was all-important as it formed the foundation for everything that was to follow. This covenant was unconditional – a promise that is going to be fulfilled.

The conditional element

In chapter 17, when Abram was 99, the whole relationship was taken further. The Lord introduced Himself to Abram as "God Almighty" – El Shaddai, further re-enforcing Abram's faith in God's ability to deliver. Here there is further reference to the covenant relationship. But this second part of the covenant was a two-way agreement. In Genesis 17 there were conditions for both parties.

- Genesis 17:4:"As for me"
  - o I will confirm my covenant with you and will greatly increase your numbers. (verse 2)
  - o You will be the father of many nations. (verse 4)
  - o No longer will you be called Abram; your name will be Abraham (father of many). (verse 5)
  - o I will make you very fruitful. (verse 6)
  - o I will make nations of you and kings will come from you. (verse 6)
  - o I will establish my covenant as an everlasting covenant between me and you and your descendants after you for the generations to come, to be your God and the God of your descendants after you. (verse 7)

- I will give them the land of Canaan as an everlasting possession to you and your descendants after you. (verse 8)
- Genesis 17:9 "As for you"
  - You must keep my covenant – and this specifically means circumcision of all males. (verses 10-13)
  - Any uncircumcised male has broken the covenant and is to be cut off from the covenant people. (verse 14)

God finishes in Genesis 17:19 by saying that He will establish his covenant with Isaac and his descendants after him.

Many of God's interactions with Abraham were to test his trust – with the final test being his willingness to sacrifice Isaac. God ended that incident by saying in Genesis 22:16

> Because you have done this and have not withheld your son, your only son, I will surely bless you and make your descendants as numerous as the stars ...

The key elements of the covenant promise are repeated because Abraham obeyed.

However, Abraham died in Genesis 26, without having seen much of the fulfilment of God's promises. He had been blessed, because he was very rich, certainly in terms of livestock. But he was still living in a tent, so there was no sign of the promise of the land being fulfilled or of him being a blessing to the whole earth. He had 6 sons by Keturah, (Genesis 25), Ishmael by Hagar and Isaac by Sarah but he was hardly a great nation.

But God confirmed His fourfold promises to Isaac (Genesis 26:3-4) and also to Jacob (Genesis 28:13-15) – the same 4 elements are still there:

- Their descendants would be a great nation.
- They would inherit the land.
- They would be blessed.
- They would be a means of blessing to the world.

But there is a further suggestion that the enjoyment of these benefits will have a condition attached. When God first made His covenant with Abram it was an unconditional promise and that still stood. But then the Lord introduced the requirement of circumcision in Genesis chapter 17.

Here in Genesis 26:4-5 the Lord said to Isaac:

> "I will make your descendants as numerous as the stars in the sky and will give them all these lands and through your offspring all nations on earth will be blessed, **because Abraham obeyed me and kept my requirements, my commands, my decrees and my laws.**"

So there is a suggestion that the fulfilment of the covenant promises depended on Abraham's obedience, and by implication, the continuing obedience of Isaac and Jacob and the children of Israel.

A question of timing

How do we make sense of this conditional/unconditional element? It seems a bit unfair to promise something and then introduce conditions later. It seems clear that the promise is certain. It will be fulfilled, but obedience is the key to *when* it is fulfilled. If Abraham's descendants did not obey, the promise could not be fulfilled at that time. Streets describes the conditional element as a "covenant within a covenant" (Ernest Streets, *The Covenants* (p12). Burch says:

God's covenant is unconditional as to the certainty of its fulfilment, but it is conditional as to its timing. (Glen Burch, *Abraham's Progress in the Covenants of God,* p9)

He continues:

> We should understand God's covenant with Abraham before this time as unbreakable and everlasting. What God was adding now was the sense of the covenant being renewed between Him and each succeeding generation ... They were to live like Abraham and walk before God as Abraham did. It was to be a continually living covenant. (*ibid.* p10)

It's really important to see this because, when the Israelites were oppressed in Egypt, as the Lord had predicted to Abram in Genesis 15:13, He showed that His covenant with Abraham was not forgotten.

> God heard their groaning and he remembered his covenant with Abraham, with Isaac and with Jacob. So God looked on the Israelites and was concerned about them.
>
> (Exodus 2:24-25)

God's response was to raise up Moses to deliver them and in Exodus 6:2-3 God said to Moses:

> "I am the Lord. I appeared to Abraham, to Isaac and Jacob as God Almighty (El Shaddai), but by my name The Lord I did not make myself known to them. I also established my covenant with them to give them the land of Canaan, where they lived as aliens. Moreover I have heard the groaning of the Israelites, whom the Egyptians are enslaving, and I have remembered my covenant."

The Lord, then, had made an unconditional promise to Abraham –
he was to be a father of nations and his descendants would have
sovereignty over the land from the river of Egypt to the Euphrates.
Israel has never owned this area in its entirety, but one day this
promise will be fulfilled. But there was a condition attaching to the
timing of it – a covenant within a covenant. The Israelites had to
follow in the Lord's ways and this was confirmed by the rite of
male circumcision, showing the people to be set apart for the Lord.
Time and again they failed to obey Him – grumbling in the
wilderness, even to the extent of making a golden calf to worship,
and following the gods of the peoples around them, when in the
land. As a result, they could not at that time enter the place of
blessing that was their destiny.

Moses led the Israelites through the wilderness until they came to
Mount Sinai. There the Lord strengthened His covenant
relationship with the people by giving them the Law. Could this
codified expression of God's will for His people encourage them
to follow in His ways and enable the promise to Abraham to
become a reality?

The Lord's Covenant with Israel at Sinai

The Lord's Covenant with Israel at Sinai

Israel's privileges and responsibility

When the Israelites arrived at the foot of Mount Sinai, Moses went up the mountain, where God told him about another covenant that He was about to make with Israel.

> "Now if you obey me fully and keep my covenant, then out of all nations you will be my treasured possession. Although the whole earth is mine, you will be for me a kingdom of priests and a holy nation." (Exodus 19:5)

Israel were to have a special position of blessing and privilege in the Lord's eyes. The Lord also revealed other blessings that He would bring upon Israel as part of His side of this further covenant. These are specifically linked with the covenant relationship in each of the following passages. The Lord would:

- Do wonders for Israel never done for any other nation (Exodus 34:10).
- Drive out before Israel all the nations in the Promised Land (Exodus 34:11).
- Increase their numbers (Leviticus 26:9).
- Give them superabundant harvests (Leviticus 26:10).
- Enable them to produce wealth (Deuteronomy 8:18).

However, all these blessings were conditional upon the nation keeping the terms of the covenant. The main requirements were contained within the Ten Commandments (which were given to Moses in Exodus 20), together with a number of other detailed instructions and decrees. The two tablets on which the Ten Commandments were written were described as "the tablets of the covenant" (Deuteronomy 9:11; see also Exodus 34:27-28). The other requirements were very detailed and covered all aspects of life. They included regulations for matters such as:

- Servants (Exodus 21).
- Personal injuries (Exodus 21).
- The protection of property and other social duties (Exodus 22).
- The kinds of food that were permissible (Deuteronomy 14).
- Justice and mercy (Exodus 23 and Deuteronomy 15).
- Sacrifices and feasts (Exodus 23 and Deuteronomy 16).

The aim of all this was to create a society that would be the envy of the world. Moses urged Israel to follow the Lord's laws carefully:

> "... for this will show your wisdom and understanding to the nations, who will hear about all these decrees and say, 'Surely this great nation is a wise and understanding people.' What other nation is so great as to have their gods near them the way the Lord our God is near us whenever we pray to him? And what other nation is so great as to have such righteous decrees and laws as this body of laws I am setting before you today?" (Deuteronomy 4:6-8)

What a vision for the people of God! If Israel had followed the Lord wholeheartedly, the potential for the Lord to enable His people not just to be blessed but also to be a means of blessing as a kingdom of priests to the other nations of the world (Exodus 19:5-6), could have been a reality at that time.

In Exodus 24 we read of the actual establishment of the covenant.

> When Moses went and told the people all the Lord's words and laws, they responded with one voice, "Everything the Lord has said we will do." (Exodus 24:3)

Animals were then sacrificed and the covenant ratified by blood.

> Moses took half of the blood and put it in bowls, and the other half he sprinkled on the altar ... Moses then took the blood, sprinkled it on the people and said, "This is the blood of the covenant[2] that the Lord has made with you in accordance with all these words." (Exodus 24:6, 8)

This covenant was a central pillar of the Lord's relationship with Israel and in this connection there were two other articles which were tangible reminders of that relationship – the Book of the Covenant and the Ark of the Covenant.

The Book of the Covenant

The detailed requirements for Israel were recorded in a book so that they would not be forgotten. After Moses had told the people the Lord's instructions and they had committed themselves to following them we read that:

> Moses then wrote down everything the Lord had said. (Exodus 24:4)

---

[2] The words used by Moses here are reminiscent of the Lord Jesus' words at the Last Supper, spoken in connection with the New Covenant, "This is my blood of the covenant, which is poured out for many." (Mark 14:24)

The people's response was repeated three verses later after Moses had sprinkled the blood on the altar.

> Then he took the Book of the Covenant and read it to the people. They responded, "We will do everything the Lord has said; we will obey." (Exodus 24:7)

Moses then sprinkled the blood on the people as evidence of their binding commitment to the covenant agreement.

The Book of the Covenant had to be kept safe but was accessible to those who administered the Law of God – the Levites.

> After Moses had finished writing in a book the words of this law from beginning to end, he gave this command to the Levites who carried the ark of covenant of the Lord: "Take this Book of the Law and place it beside the ark of the covenant of the Lord your God. There it will remain as a witness against you." (Deuteronomy 31:24-26)

Moses was succeeded by Joshua and, towards the end of his life, his final act was to renew the covenant made with Moses and to record the decrees in the Book of the Law of God. He first reminded Israel again of the Lord's blessing to them in bringing them up from Egypt and settling them in the land, driving out the nations before them. He also repeated the warnings to Israel not to follow other gods.

> On that day Joshua made a covenant for the people and there at Shechem he drew up for them decrees and laws. And Joshua recorded these things in the Book of the Law of God. Then he took a large stone and set it up there under the oak near the holy place of the Lord. (Joshua 24:25-26)

Generations later, at the height of Judah's apostasy, Josiah came to the throne. He tried to follow the Lord and when he set about repairing the temple the Book of the Covenant was found there and formed the basis for a genuine (though sadly temporary) repentance of the people – see pages 46-47 below.

The Ark of the Covenant

The Ark of the Covenant was a chest of acacia wood (Exodus 25:10), made in accordance with detailed instructions given by the Lord to Moses in Exodus 25. The Ark was to be carried by the Levites (Deuteronomy 10:8) using poles.[3]

Into the Ark were placed the two tablets containing the Ten Commandments (Deuteronomy 10:1-5), Aaron's rod and a pot of manna (Hebrews 9:4). The Ark was generally kept in the Tabernacle but was carried before the people as they travelled (Numbers 10:33) and when they went into battle (e.g. at Jericho in Joshua 6). The Ark was therefore a symbol of the Lord's presence with the people and His special covenant relationship with them. The Ark appeared to possess powers of its own as the Philistines discovered when they captured it and placed it in the temple of their god, Dagon. (See 1 Samuel chapter 5.)

David eventually brought the Ark to Jerusalem with a great celebration (1 Chronicles 15) and placed it inside a tent (1 Chronicles 16:1). He appointed Levites to minister before the Ark (1 Chronicles 16:4) and instructed Solomon to place the Ark in the

---

[3] When the ark was being transported in a cart to Jerusalem by David, the oxen pulling the cart stumbled. Uzzah put his hand on the ark to steady it and died as a result. (2 Samuel 6:6-7)

temple that he was going to build (1 Chronicles 22:19), which he eventually did (2 Chronicles 5:2-10).

The Ark of the Covenant and the Book of the Covenant were important symbols of the relationship between the Lord and Israel and were designed to keep reminding Israel of the nature of that relationship. If they followed the Lord's instructions, He in turn would bless them and fulfil His promises to them; if they turned away from Him, the punishments they had been warned about would come upon them (see Deuteronomy 28 for the blessings and the punishments).

The detailed requirements governing the life of the nation were not all given to them at Sinai. In Deuteronomy 29:1 we read of Moses renewing the covenant in Moab, "in addition to the covenant he made with them at Horeb (Sinai)". This renewal reminded the people of how God enabled them to survive in the wilderness without their clothes wearing out (Deuteronomy 29:5) and warned them not to be seduced into following the gods of the nations around them (Deuteronomy 29:18).

The relationship of this covenant to the Abrahamic covenant

The Lord's instructions given to Israel as part of the Mosaic covenant were much more detailed and specific than anything that had been said to Abraham, Isaac and Jacob. They covered the whole social, religious and political life of the nation. Yet in a sense they were a development from the earlier covenant. The same principle applied: as with the Abrahamic covenant, the future blessing of Israel was assured. It was only the timing of it that was uncertain. If the people followed the Lord's instructions the blessing would soon follow. If they did not, there would be a delay.

This was demonstrated in the fact that the nation was condemned to wander in the wilderness for forty years, until the adult generation that had come out of Egypt had all died (Numbers 14:20-25). The delay was due to their failure to trust in the Lord.

This principle is clearly set out in Leviticus 26, where the Lord promised the people prosperity and peace if they obey Him, but went on to warn them of the devastating punishments He would inflict on them for disobedience; they would suffer illness (verse 16), their enemies would overcome them (verse 17), their crops would fail (verse 20), a vast number of them would be wiped out (verses 27-31), and ultimately they would go into exile (verse 33). Then He paused and set before them the hope of eventual restoration.

> But if they will confess their sins and the sins of their fathers ... I will remember my covenant with Jacob and my covenant with Isaac and my covenant with Abraham, and I will remember the land ... when they are in the land of their enemies I will not reject them or abhor them so as to destroy them completely, breaking my covenant with them. I am the Lord their God. (Leviticus 26:40-45)

In the early part of Deuteronomy, as he explained the Ten Commandments to the people, Moses pointed out the connection between this further covenant and the original promises to Abraham.

> It was because the Lord loved you and kept the oath he swore to your forefathers that he brought you out with a mighty hand and redeemed you from the power of slavery ... Know that the Lord your God is God; he is the faithful God, keeping his covenant of love to a thousand generations of those who love him and keep his commands

... If you pay attention to these laws and are careful to follow them, then the Lord your God will keep his covenant of love with you, as he swore to your forefathers. (Deuteronomy 7:8-12)

In Moab also, where the Lord supplemented the covenant made at Sinai, there is reference back to His dealings with Abraham:

Carefully follow the terms of this covenant, so that you may prosper in everything you do ... You are standing here in order to enter into a covenant with the Lord your God, a covenant the Lord is making with you this day and sealing with an oath, to confirm you this day as his people, that he may be your God as he promised you and as he swore to your fathers, Abraham, Isaac and Jacob. (Deuteronomy 29:9-13)

The covenant at Sinai, then, did not replace the covenant made with Abraham, Isaac and Jacob. Instead, it fleshed out in greater detail the Lord's expectations for a people who were to be His prized possession, a kingdom of priests administering His blessings to the world. But the establishment of this more detailed covenant did not prove to be any more of an incentive to the nation to follow the Lord wholeheartedly.

The danger of idolatry

The main temptation the Israelites faced as they prepared to move into the land was the danger of turning from the Lord, to follow the gods of the people among whom they were living, and whom the Lord had promised to drive out before them.

Repeatedly, Moses warned the people of the consequences of idolatry. For example:

Be careful not to forget the covenant of the Lord your God that he made with you; do not make for yourselves an idol ... if you then become corrupt and make any kind of idol, doing evil in the eyes of the Lord your God and provoking him to anger ... you will certainly be destroyed. (Deuteronomy 4:23-26)

As he prepared to die, Moses was under no illusions about what was likely to happen:

For I know that after my death you are sure to become utterly corrupt and to turn from the way I have commanded you. In days to come, disaster will fall upon you because you will do evil in the sight of the Lord and provoke him to anger by what your hands have made. (Deuteronomy 31:29)

Joshua, too, in his farewell to the people, warned them of the dangers of following other gods.

If you violate the covenant of the Lord your God, which he commanded you and go and serve other gods and bow down to them, the Lord's anger will burn against you and you will quickly perish from the good land he has given you. (Joshua 23:16)

History tells us that these concerns were justified. Throughout the period of the Judges, who succeeded Joshua, a depressing pattern emerged:

- the Israelites committed idolatry;
- they were then oppressed by the peoples around them in the land;
- they cried out to the Lord in their suffering;
- He sent a judge to deliver them;

- they returned to worshipping the Lord for a time before slipping back into their old ways.

Judges 2 explains the position:

> When the judge died, the people returned to ways even more corrupt than those of their fathers, following other gods and worshipping them ... Therefore the Lord was angry with Israel and said, "Because this nation has violated the covenant that I laid down for their forefathers and has not listened to me, I will no longer drive out before them any of the nations Joshua left when he died." (Judges 2:19-21)

Because Israel had not followed the Lord, the Canaanite nations remained in the land and were a source of trouble to them in the years to come.

This sad situation continued until the Lord raised up Samuel the prophet and the kingdom was established through Saul. However, it was not until David came to the throne that the Lord took His covenant relationship with Israel further by establishing a covenant with him.

The Lord's Covenant with David

The Lord's Covenant with David

In 1 Chronicles 10 and 11 we read of the death of Saul and the establishment of David as king over Israel. As countrywide support grew, he was installed in Jerusalem and the Ark of the Covenant brought there. David sang a Psalm of thanks to the Lord for all His blessings, including His promise of the land to Abraham, Isaac and Jacob (1 Chronicles 16:15-18). After he was settled in his palace David told the prophet Nathan that he intended to build a temple in Jerusalem for the Lord. Although Nathan initially approved of David's decision, the Lord soon told him otherwise.

1 Chronicles 17 records Nathan's report to David of what the Lord had told him. The key points are:

- The Lord reminded David that He had never asked for a temple to be built all the time He had been with Israel since they came out of Egypt. Instead, the Lord had been content to dwell in a tent (verses 4-6).
- David had been raised up by the Lord to be ruler of Israel (verse 7). The Lord had destroyed David's enemies and He was now going to make David's name great in all the earth (verse 8).
- Israel will be established in the land and will not be disturbed (verses 9-10).
- The Lord will raise up David's offspring to succeed him and He will establish his kingdom (verse 11). He is the one who will build the temple (verse 12).
- His throne will be established forever and God will never take His love away from him (verse 13).

Although the word "covenant" is not used in 1 Chronicles 17, there is no doubt that a covenant relationship had been established. Towards the end of his life, David spoke a final oracle in which he said:

> Is not my house right with God? Has he not made with me an everlasting covenant, arranged and secured in every part? Will he not bring to fruition my salvation and grant me my every desire? (2 Samuel 23:5)

In the Psalms, too, we read of the covenant the Lord made with David. For example:

> You said, "I have made a covenant with my chosen one, I have sworn to David my servant, 'I will establish your line forever and make your throne firm through all generations.'"... Once for all, I have sworn by my holiness – and I will not lie to David – that his line will continue forever and his throne before me like the sun; it will be established like the moon, the faithful witness in the sky. (Psalm 89:3-4, 35-37)

So this is a covenant comprising an unconditional promise that Solomon's throne will be established forever and that God will never take His love away from him. However, as in the case of the earlier covenant with Israel, although the ultimate outcome is certain, the timing of the fulfilment of the promise could be affected by any disobedience to the Lord's commands. Psalm 89 is written against a background of Israel being oppressed and recognises that the fulfilment of the unconditional covenant to David and his line depends on their obedience to the Lord.

> "If his sons forsake my law and do not follow my statutes, if they violate my decrees and fail to keep my commands, I will punish their sin with the rod, their iniquity with

flogging; but I will not take my love from him, nor will I ever betray my faithfulness. I will not violate my covenant, or alter what my lips have uttered. (Psalm 89:30-34)

Therefore it is clear that, in spite of Israel's disobedience, the covenant relationship still stands, and Psalm 89 ends with a plea to the Lord to remember His covenant with David and to come out of "hiding" to deliver His people. Similar ideas can also be found in Psalm 132.

David's instructions to Solomon

David recognised the danger that Solomon was in. The full implementation of the covenant was contingent on obedience. When he was discussing his plans for the temple with his royal officials he reported the Lord's words to him.

> He said to me: "Solomon your son is the one who will build my house and my courts, for I have chosen him to be my son, and I will be his father. I will establish his kingdom forever **if he is unswerving in carrying out my commands and laws**, as is being done at this time." (1 Chronicles 28:6-7)

David then went on to impress on Solomon the importance of continuing to follow the Lord wholeheartedly and, initially, Solomon appeared to take his father's words to heart. In 2 Chronicles 1, we find the famous incident where he asked the Lord for wisdom rather than power or glory and was rewarded with all of these. After Solomon built the temple the Lord appeared to him and repeated the warnings:

> As for you, if you walk before me as David your father did and do all I command and observe my decrees and laws, I

will establish your royal throne, as I covenanted with David your father when I said, "You shall never fail to have a man to rule over Israel." But if you turn away and forsake the decrees and commands I have given you and go off to serve other gods and to worship them, then I will uproot Israel from my land which I have given them, and will reject this temple I have consecrated for my Name. (2 Chronicles 7:17-20)

So there we have a chilling warning about the exile which, sadly, eventually came to pass. Solomon, having started well, was soon diverted away from the Lord by the foreign wives he had married (1 Kings 11:1-4) and started to worship Ashtoreth and Molech, the detestable god of the Ammonites.

The Lord became angry with Solomon because his heart had turned away from the Lord, the God of Israel ...Although he had forbidden Solomon to follow other gods, Solomon did not keep the Lord's command. So the Lord said to Solomon, "Since this is your attitude ... I will most certainly tear the kingdom away from you and give it to one of your subordinates. Nevertheless, for the sake of David your father, I will not do it during your lifetime. I will tear it out of the hand of your son." (1 Kings 11:9-12)

So here again, history was repeating itself. Israel the nation had failed to follow the Lord fully and, as a result, had not been able to come into full possession of the Promised Land. Other nations, whom the Lord had intended to drive out before them, were still there and caused problems. Now Solomon, who could have had an unbroken line of succession after him, had forfeited this because of his idolatry. What was to happen to the nation now?

The Nation after Solomon

The Nation after Solomon

Solomon's son Rehoboam succeeded him and, during his reign, the nation was divided into two separate houses - Israel (the northern kingdom) and Judah (the southern kingdom). Thereafter there was a succession of kings in both kingdoms who either followed the Lord (and were victorious) or worshipped Canaanite gods (and were defeated). 2 Kings 17:13-15 sums up the position.

> The Lord warned Israel and Judah through all his prophets and seers: "Turn from your evil ways. Observe my commands and decrees, in accordance with the entire Law that I commanded your fathers to obey and that I delivered to you through my servants the prophets." But they would not listen and were as stiff-necked as their fathers, who did not trust in the Lord their God. They rejected his decrees and the covenant he had made with their fathers and the warnings he had given them.

The historic books

In the historic books of the Old Testament we find periodic references to the covenants. For example, Elijah, on the run from Ahab and Jezebel, complained to the Lord:

> The Israelites have rejected your covenant, broken down your altars and put your prophets to death with the sword. (1 Kings 19:10)

Much later, the Lord caused Hazael, king of Aram, to oppress Israel throughout the reign of the evil king Jehoahaz. However, we then read that:

> ... the Lord was gracious to them and had compassion and showed concern for them because of his covenant with Abraham, Isaac and Jacob. To this day he has been unwilling to destroy them or banish them from his presence. (2 Kings 13:23)

Four chapters later, we read of the exile of Israel into Assyria, because of their idolatry. 2 Kings 17:15 states:

> They rejected his decrees and the covenant he had made with their fathers and the warnings he had given them. They followed worthless idols and themselves became worthless.

Which covenant does this refer to? The answer is given in chapter 18:

> This happened because they had not obeyed the Lord their God, but had violated his covenant – all that Moses the servant of the Lord commanded. They neither listened to his commands nor carried them out. (2 Kings 18:12)

Thus, there appears to be a coming together of the Abrahamic and the Mosaic covenants. The idolatry and general disobedience of Israel had broken both covenants and had resulted in the realisation of the punishments the Lord had warned them about. The nation was divided into two and one part had been exiled.

Judah managed to hold out a little longer. In 2 Kings 22 we read of the eight year old king Josiah.

> He did what was right in the eyes of the Lord and walked
> in all the ways of his father David. (2 Kings 22:2)

It is interesting that this good king is described as walking in the ways of David, suggesting a connection with the Lord's covenant relationship with David. Josiah decided to repair the temple and, when the work started they discovered the Book of the Law. This ancient book had been forgotten and, when Josiah heard what was in it, he was horrified because the people had not been obeying it. (See 2 Kings 22:11-13.)

So he gathered all the elders together in Jerusalem:

> He read in their hearing all the words of the Book of the
> Covenant, which had been found in the temple of the Lord.
> The king stood by the pillar and renewed the covenant in
> the presence of the Lord – to follow the Lord and keep his
> commands, regulations and decrees with all his heart and
> all his soul, thus confirming the words of the covenant
> written in the book. Then all the people pledged themselves
> to the covenant. (2 Kings 23:2-3)

Again, although this refers primarily to the covenant at Sinai, it can be interpreted more generally as the wider covenant relationship between the Lord and His people – a nation seeking to obey Him, under the leadership of a godly king in David's line.

Unfortunately, Josiah's successors did not follow their father's example and in a short time they too were exiled – taken into Babylon by King Nebuchadnezzar.

The prophetic writings

The prophets also pleaded with both houses of Israel not to break their covenant and pronounced the Lord's judgment on them for doing so. For example:

Prophets preaching to the house of Israel

> "Put the trumpet to your lips! An eagle is over the house of the Lord because the people have broken my covenant and rebelled against my law. Israel cries out to me, 'O our God, we acknowledge you!' But Israel has rejected what is good; an enemy will pursue him." (Hosea 8:1-3)

> "Hear this word the Lord has spoken against you, O people of Israel – against the whole family I brought up out of Egypt: You only have I chosen of all the families of the earth; therefore I will punish you for all your sins." (Amos 3:1-2)

Prophets preaching to the house of Judah

> "From the time I brought your forefathers up from Egypt until today, I warned them again and again, saying, 'Obey me.' But they did not listen or pay attention; instead they followed the stubbornness of their evil hearts. So I brought on them all the curses of the covenant I had commanded them to follow but that they did not keep." (Jeremiah 11:7-8)

> "This is what the Sovereign Lord says: 'As surely as I live, I will bring down on his head my oath that he despised and my covenant that he broke. I will spread my net for him and he will be caught in my snare. I will bring him to Babylon

and execute judgment upon him there because he was unfaithful to me.'" (Ezekiel 17:19-20)

Yet, in spite of this, the ultimate hope of restoration to the land and the re-unification of both houses still remains:

"Return, O Israel, to the Lord your God. Your sins have been your downfall ... I will heal their waywardness and love them freely, for my anger has turned away from them." (Hosea 14:1,4)

"In that day I will restore David's fallen tent. I will repair its broken places and restore its ruins ... I will plant Israel in their own land, never again to be uprooted from the land I have given them," says the Lord your God. (Amos 9:11,15)

"The days are coming," declares the Lord, "when I will bring my people Israel and Judah back from captivity and restore them to the land I gave their forefathers to possess," says the Lord. (Jeremiah 30:3)

"This is what the Sovereign Lord says: 'I will take the Israelites out of the nations where they have gone. I will gather them from all around and bring them back into their own land. I will make them one nation in the land, on the mountains of Israel. There will be one king over all of them and they will never again be two nations or be divided into two kingdoms. They will no longer defile themselves with their idols and vile images or with any of their offences, for I will save them from all their sinful backsliding and I will cleanse them. They will be my people, and I will be their God.'" (Ezekiel 37:21-23)

The people restored to the land

Jeremiah had predicted that Judah's exile to Babylon would last for seventy years, after which Babylon would be punished for its sins (Jeremiah 25:11-12). 2 Chronicles closes with the announcement of the restoration of Judah as the Lord moved the heart of Cyrus, who had conquered Babylon, to arrange for Jerusalem to be rebuilt. The books of Ezra and Nehemiah record how these plans were accomplished. It is important to note the important place the covenant relationship and the Law of Moses has in the returning nation.

In Babylon, Nehemiah pleaded with the Lord for the restoration of the nation, reminding Him of His covenant promise to restore the nation if they repent.

> "O Lord God of heaven, the great and awesome God, who keeps his covenant of love with those who love him and obey his commands, let your ear be attentive and your eyes open to hear the prayer your servant is praying before you day and night for your servants, the people of Israel ...We have acted very wickedly toward you. We have not obeyed the commands, decrees and laws you gave your servant Moses ... Remember the instruction you gave your servant Moses, saying ... if you return to me and obey my commands, then even if your exiled people are at the farthest horizon, I will gather them from there and bring them to the place I have chosen as a dwelling for my Name." (Nehemiah 1:5-9)

The exiles began to return; Nehemiah supervised the building of the city walls. The altar of the Lord was rebuilt and work was started on rebuilding the temple (Ezra 3). Ezra, who was a teacher well-versed in the Law of Moses (Ezra 7:6), came up to Jerusalem from Babylon and began to teach the people:

> Ezra had devoted himself to the study and observance of the Law of the Lord, and to teaching its decrees and laws in Israel. (Ezra 7:10)

In Nehemiah 9, we read of the Israelite people standing to worship the Lord, declaring the Lord's past blessings on the nation throughout their history, including reference to the covenant made with Abraham (verses 7-8), and the giving of the Law to Moses (verses 13-14). The people confessed their failings, and those of their forefathers and created a binding agreement (covenant) to follow the Law of God (verse 38).

But all was not well. Malachi, who prophesied around this time, criticised the people for half-hearted obedience to the Lord, and for only going through the motions of worship, by bringing lame and diseased animals for sacrifice.

> "You profane (my name) by saying of the Lord's table, 'It is defiled' and of its food, 'It is contemptible.' And you say. 'What a burden!' and you sniff at it contemptuously," says the Lord Almighty. (Malachi 1:12,13)

So how was the restoration of the nation both to the land and to the Lord to be accomplished? They were back in the land, chastened by their experiences in exile, but their following of the Lord was reluctant and unenthusiastic. Could the covenants be put into effect?

In summary ...

The covenant with Abraham and the covenant with Moses are essentially regarded as part of the same relationship between the Lord and His people. The Lord's purpose was to bless Abraham's descendants by giving them a land and prosperity. He also showed Abraham that He wanted to use this chosen nation as a kingdom of priests to bring His blessing on the world. The covenant with Moses was a more detailed expression of the same purpose. The realisation of this purpose depended on the obedience of the people.

The implementation of the covenant with David added a further dimension – the chosen nation was to be led by a king in David's line. But again the realisation of this depended on obedience – in this case of both king and nation.

But Israel's history was one of failure. Both houses of Israel had been in exile and, although some of the exiles had returned with Nehemiah, and worship of the Lord had resumed, the writings of Malachi show that the situation was far from ideal. How was this situation to be resolved so that the unconditional elements of all the covenant promises could be fulfilled?

The answer is that some of the prophets caught a vision of something new – something greater than had been revealed before – that God would introduce a new covenant that would unite the houses of Israel, and write His laws on the hearts of the people. This vision will be explored in the next section.

The New Covenant in the Old Testament

The New Covenant in the Old Testament

The vision of the prophets

Several of the Old Testament prophets foresaw the means by which the Lord would fulfil His covenant promises to Israel. This section will concentrate on the message of five of these prophets – Isaiah, Jeremiah, Ezekiel, Joel and Zechariah.

All five prophets spoke to the people of Judah. Isaiah and Jeremiah both prophesied before the exile into Babylon. Isaiah started around 650BC and prophesied during the reigns of kings Uzziah, Jotham, Ahaz and Hezekiah (Isaiah 1:1). Jeremiah began around 130 years later during the reigns of kings Josiah, Jehoiakim and Zedekiah, right up to the time the people of Judah went into exile (Jeremiah 1:2-3). Ezekiel commenced his prophetic ministry from exile in Babylon (Ezekiel 1:1-3) around 485BC and ended shortly before Nehemiah started to bring the people back to the land. Joel gives no indication of when his prophecy was written but many think it was written just before or just after the Babylonian captivity. Finally, Zechariah, one of the last of the Old Testament prophets, operated after the captivity, over a seven year period from 410-403BC.[4]

---

[4] For a discussion of the dates and inter-relationships between the prophets and kings of Israel and Judah, see *Prophets, Kings & Chronicles* by Michael Penny.

All of these prophets foresaw a restoration, not only of Judah to the land, but a re-unification of both houses of Israel. United Israel would follow the ways of the Lord wholeheartedly because, by His Spirit, He would write their laws on their hearts and they would all know and serve Him. Thus the conditions for the fulfilment of the Abrahamic and the Mosaic covenants would be created.

Not only so, but the newly united people of God would be ruled by a king in David's line, who would perfectly follow the Lord's ways. In this way the Davidic covenant could be fulfilled and God's purposes could be carried to their glorious conclusion.

That is the message of these prophets in a nutshell but what of the detail? The next section traces the prophetic revelation and explores the principal aspects.

The promise of restoration

Jeremiah, while predicting God's punishment on faithless Judah, foresaw the day when their misfortunes would be reversed.

> "The days are coming," declares the Lord, "when I will bring my people Israel and Judah back from captivity and restore them to the land I gave their forefathers to possess," says the Lord. (Jeremiah 30:3)

There we can see a reference to the original promise to Abraham, Isaac and Jacob that they would be given the land. Ezekiel, too, predicted the reuniting of the kingdoms under one king

> This is what the Sovereign Lord says: "I will take the Israelites out of the nations where they have gone. I will gather them from all around and bring them back into their own land. I will make them one nation in the land on the

mountains of Israel. There will be one king over all of them and they will never again be two nations or be divided into two kingdoms." (Ezekiel 37:20-22)

Zechariah pictured the Lord reigning in Jerusalem:

> The Lord will inherit Judah as his portion in the holy land and will again choose Jerusalem ... This is what the Lord says: "I will return to Zion and dwell in Jerusalem. Then Jerusalem will be called the City of Truth and the mountain of the Lord Almighty will be called the Holy Mountain." (Zechariah 2:12; 8:3)

The new covenant

These three passages give a flavour of the restored, faithful Israel, righteous and united under a single king. But how would this be accomplished? By a new and very different covenant. Jeremiah spelled out the details:

> "The time is coming," declares the Lord, "when I will make a new covenant with the house of Israel and with the house of Judah. It will not be like the covenant I made with their forefathers when I took them by the hand to lead them out of Egypt, because they broke my covenant ... This is the covenant I will make with the house of Israel after that time," declares the Lord. "I will put my law in their minds and write it on their hearts. I will be their God and they will be my people. No longer will a man teach his neighbour, or a man his brother, saying, 'Know the Lord,' because they will all know me, from the least of them to the greatest," declares the Lord. "For I will forgive their wickedness and will remember their sins no more." (Jeremiah 31:32-34)

The people of Israel and Judah had not been able to keep the Law, as was required under the old, Mosaic covenant. They had had bursts of enthusiasm from time to time but had not been able to sustain it. Something much more fundamental was required – a complete internal transformation - and here in Jeremiah 31 the Lord promises to put His law into their minds and write it on their hearts. This was to be a work of the Holy Spirit, as Isaiah and Ezekiel explain:

> "As for me, this is my covenant with them," says the Lord, "My Spirit, who is on you, and my words that I have put in your mouth will not depart from your mouth, or the mouths of your children, or from the mouths of their descendants from this time on and forever," says the Lord. (Isaiah 59:20-21)

> "I will take you out of the nations; I will gather you from all the countries and bring you back into your own land...I will give you a new heart and put a new spirit in you ... And I will put my Spirit in you and move you to follow my decrees and be careful to keep my laws. You will live in the land I gave your forefathers; you will be my people, and I will be your God." (Ezekiel 36:24, 26-28)

> "I will put my Spirit in you and you will live, and I will settle you in your own land. Then you will know that I the Lord have spoken, and that I have done it," declares the Lord. (Ezekiel 37:14)

Isaiah 59:20-21 specifically links the permanent presence of the indwelling Spirit with the (new) covenant. The people of reunited Israel from generation to generation will be hard-wired to follow the ways of the Lord through the work of His Spirit within them.

The coming of the Spirit is also a feature of Joel. He described the Lord's restoration of Israel and declared:

> And afterward, I will pour out my Spirit on all people. Your sons and daughters will prophesy, your old men will dream dreams, your young men will see visions. Even on my servants, both men and women, I will pour out my Spirit in those days ... And everyone who calls on the name of the Lord will be saved; for on Mount Zion and in Jerusalem there will be deliverance, as the Lord has said, among the survivors whom the Lord calls. (Joel 2:28-32)

The new covenant to be established will never come to an end. Isaiah, Jeremiah and Ezekiel all describe it as an "everlasting covenant".

> "In those days, at that time," declares the Lord, "the people of Israel and the people of Judah together will go in tears to seek the Lord their God. They will ask the way to Zion and turn their faces toward it. They will come and bind themselves to the Lord in an **everlasting covenant** that will not be forgotten." (Jeremiah 50:4-5)

> This is what the Sovereign Lord says: "I will deal with you as you deserve, because you have despised my oath by breaking the covenant. Yet I will remember the covenant I made with you in the days of your youth, and I will establish an **everlasting covenant** with you." (Ezekiel 16:59-60)

> Give ear and come to me; hear me, that your soul may live. I will make an **everlasting covenant** with you, my faithful love promised to David. (Isaiah 55:3)

The king reigning over the united nation

This covenant, unlike the covenants with Abraham and Moses, will not fail because of Israel's inability to obey the Lord since His law will be written on their hearts, by the Holy Spirit. However, Isaiah 55:3, quoted above, states that this "everlasting covenant" is the expression of the Lord's faithful love to David – set out in the Davidic covenant. And the new, everlasting covenant is the means by which the Lord's promises to David will be fulfilled.

David had been promised that if his sons followed in the Lord's ways he would never fail to have a descendant to sit on his throne (2 Chronicles 7:18). Unfortunately the kings of Israel and Judah, like their people, had turned their backs on the Lord and suffered as a consequence. But the vision of the prophets was for the coming of a descendant of David who would follow the Lord perfectly, and reign as king over the nation. One of the titles given to this coming king is "the Branch."

> A shoot will come up from the stump of Jesse; from his roots a Branch will bear fruit. The Spirit of the Lord will rest on him – the Spirit of wisdom and of understanding, the Spirit of counsel and of power, the Spirit of knowledge and of the fear of the Lord – and he will delight in the fear of the Lord.. (Isaiah 11:1-3)

Here in Isaiah we have a vision of a righteous and just leadership, and the remainder of Isaiah 11 spells out the glories of Israel under His leadership.

Jeremiah also foresaw His coming:

> "The days are coming," declares the Lord, "when I will raise up to David a righteous Branch, a King who will reign

wisely and do what is just and right in the land. In his days Judah will be saved and Israel will live in safety. This is the name by which he will be called: The Lord Our Righteousness." (Jeremiah 23:5-6; see also Jeremiah 33:14-16)

The coming of the Branch was also revealed to Zechariah, but he went further than Isaiah and Jeremiah, revealing the Branch as a priest as well as a king. This is extraordinary as these two offices were never combined in Israel – the kings came from the tribe of Judah and the priests from Levi. Yet the Branch will bring them together:

> This is what the Lord Almighty says: "Here is the man whose name is the Branch, and he will branch out from his place and build the temple of the Lord ... And he will be a priest on his throne. And there will be harmony between the two." (Zechariah 6:12-13)

So we can see the picture coming together. Interestingly, Ezekiel saw Israel's coming king not just as a descendant of David, but as David himself, raised from the dead to rule over Israel.

> My servant David will be king over them and they will all have one shepherd. They will follow my laws and be careful to keep my decrees... They and their children and their children's children will live there forever and David my servant will be their prince forever. I will make a covenant of peace with them; it will be an everlasting covenant... (Ezekiel 37:24-25. See also Ezekiel 34:23-24)

Here is an intriguing possibility. Will the resurrected David indeed rule again over Israel on a permanent basis? Or is Ezekiel merely speaking figuratively of David's descendant? The passages announcing the coming king do suggest that someone much greater than David is in mind.

The blessing of the land

What a wonderful time this will be for the people of Israel – the covenants fulfilled; the nation, restored and worshipping the Lord wholeheartedly; ruled by a righteous king in David's line (or David himself?); the Lord making His dwelling among His people in Jerusalem. The concluding chapters of Isaiah are full of poetic pictures of this glorious time, but other prophets also shared in the vision. For example:

> You will go out in joy and be led forth in peace; the mountains and hills will burst into song before you, and all the trees of the field will clap their hands. Instead of the thornbush will grow the pine tree, and instead of briers the myrtle will grow. This will be for the Lord's renown, for an everlasting sign, which will not be destroyed. (Isaiah 55:12-13)

> This is what the Lord Almighty says: "Once again men and women of ripe old age will sit in the streets of Jerusalem, each with cane in hand because of his age. The city will be filled with boys and girls playing there. (Zechariah 8:4-5).

Zechariah 8 sums up the situation by saying:

> This is what the Lord Almighty says: "In those days ten men from all languages and nations will take hold of one Jew by the hem of his robe and say, 'Let us go with you, because we have heard that God is with you.'" (Zechariah 8:23)

Is this actually going to happen?

What a marvellous vision this is for the future of Israel! But is it something that is going to happen or is it just a poetic way of expressing a *potential* future for the nation? Some scholars have argued that prophecy is not "history written in advance" but more a kind of vision of one possible future among many, if the people do certain things and refrain from doing other things. In fact, it is argued, all that we read of here has been superseded by later events and God's purposes have moved on.

The problem with this view is that in many of the passages quoted above, we find phrases like:

- "This is what the Sovereign Lord says..."
- "This is what the Lord Almighty says...
- "... declares the Lord..."

Phrases like this are intended to re-enforce the certainty of what is to come. They have the backing, not just of the prophet's visionary mind, but of the Lord, who is Sovereign and Almighty and who makes declarations.

In addition to this, it is worth noting that there are places where the Lord goes out of His way to emphasise the certainty of these coming events. For example:

> This is what the Lord says: "Only if the heavens above can be measured and the foundations of the earth below be searched out will I reject all the descendants of Israel because of what they have done," declares the Lord. (Jeremiah 31:37)

This is what the Lord says: "If I have not established my covenant with day and night and the fixed laws of heaven and earth, then I will reject the descendants of Jacob and David my servant and I will not choose one of his sons to rule over the descendants of Abraham, Isaac and Jacob." (Jeremiah 33:25-26)

If we remember that God knows the future, then it is hardly credible that the God of Truth would make such statements, knowing, as He said them, that these events would never come to pass.

Therefore it is hard to see how the Lord could make it clearer: This is going to happen!

But how? ... And who? ... And when? ...

Isaiah, as we have seen, proclaimed the coming blessings on Israel, when the new covenant will be established and the king will reign. Taking upon himself the voice of the coming One he declared:

The Spirit of the Sovereign Lord is upon me, because the Lord has anointed me to preach good news to the poor. He has sent me to bind up the brokenhearted, to proclaim freedom for the captives and release from darkness for the prisoners, to proclaim the year of the Lord's favour ...(Isaiah 61:1-2).

Some 650 years later a young man – the son of the village carpenter, stood up in His local synagogue to read the Scriptures. It was this passage in Isaiah that was the reading for the day. Isaiah's proclamation continues beyond verse 2 to speak of the day of vengeance of our God, but the young Jesus stopped the reading after proclaiming the year of the Lord's favour, rolled up the scroll and sat down. And the eyes of everyone were fastened on Him (Luke 4:20).

Stopping the reading in mid-sentence was surprising enough but then He said:

> "Today this scripture is fulfilled in your hearing." (Luke 4:21)

The circumstances for the potential fulfilment of the Lord's promises had arrived and the next section explores the references to the new covenant in the New Testament.

The New Covenant in the New Testament

The New Covenant in the New Testament

Although the word "covenant" occurs 21 times in the epistle to the Hebrews, it is infrequently used elsewhere in the New Testament. Despite the title to the second part of the Scriptures, the new covenant does not pervade our New Testament.

The only references to the new covenant in the Gospels are found during the last supper, when the Lord Jesus celebrated the final Passover with His disciples. The incident occurs in three of the Gospels – in Matthew 26, Mark 14 and Luke 22. There are no references to the new covenant in John's Gospel or the book of Acts and in Paul's epistles, only Romans 11, 1 Corinthians 11 and 2 Corinthians 3 speak of a future covenant. The phrase does not appear in any of the epistles of Peter, James, Jude and John.

It is only when we turn to the epistle to the Hebrews that we find a detailed exposition of the new covenant and an explanation of how the work of Christ creates the conditions for the introduction of the new covenant for His people.

Christ the fulfiller

When the Lord Jesus, in the synagogue in Nazareth, applied Isaiah's prophecy to Himself, He was declaring Himself to be the One of whom the prophets had spoken – the Lord's anointed One preaching deliverance, the Son of David, the bringer of the Holy Spirit into the hearts and minds of the people. Isaiah, foreseeing the time when the Lord would return to save Israel, declared:

Then will the eyes of the blind be opened and the ears of the deaf unstopped. Then will the lame leap like a deer and the mute tongue shout for joy. (Isaiah 35:5-6)

Throughout His ministry the Lord Jesus went out of His way to show His credentials:

- His miracles of healing and His words of comfort and wisdom identified Him as the subject of Isaiah's prophecy. When John the Baptist, in prison and in despair, sent his disciples to ask Jesus if He really was the One they were waiting for, the Lord's reply emphasised these aspects.

  Jesus replied, "Go back and report to John what you hear and see: The blind receive sight, the lame walk, those who have leprosy are cured, the deaf hear, the dead are raised and the good news is preached to the poor. Blessed is the man who does not fall away on account of me." (Matthew 11:4-6)

- The identity of the Lord Jesus as Son of David, and therefore king of Israel, is also clearly identified. Matthew opens with His genealogy showing His direct descent from both Abraham and David. Some of the people He healed addressed Him as "Son of David" (e.g. Matthew 9:27; 15:22; Luke 18:38). When He rode into Jerusalem on a donkey He did this to fulfil the prophecy of Zechariah:

  "Say to the Daughter of Zion, 'See your king comes to you, gentle and riding on a donkey, on a colt, the foal of a donkey.'" (Matthew 21:5).

The crowds surrounding Him as he approached the city realised this and shouted:

"Hosanna to the Son of David! Blessed is he who comes in the name of the Lord!" (Matthew 21:9)

The Pharisees were scandalised but Jesus endorsed what was being said:

> But when the chief priests and the teachers of the law saw the wonderful things he did and the children shouting in the temple area, "Hosanna to the Son of David," they were indignant. "Do you hear what these children are saying?" they asked him. "Yes," Jesus replied, "have you never read, 'From the lips of children and infants you have ordained praise'?" (Matthew 21:15-16)

- When Jesus met the woman at the well, He told her that:

> "Everyone who drinks this water will be thirsty again, but whoever drinks the water I give him will never thirst. Indeed the water I give him will become in him a spring of water, welling up to eternal life." (John 4:13-14)

His meaning is not altogether clear, although it does seem to have some connection with "worship in spirit and truth" (John 4:23-24). However, in John 7, we read that on the last day of the Feast of Tabernacles, Jesus stood up and declared:

> If anyone is thirsty, let him come to me and drink. Whoever believes in me, as the Scripture has said, streams of living water will flow from within him. (John 7:37-38)

Again, this is rather obscure but John immediately adds the explanation:

By this he meant the Spirit, whom those who believed in him were to receive. Up to that time the Spirit had not been given, since Jesus had not yet been glorified. (John 7:39)

So the scene was being set for the implementation of the new covenant. But the Spirit could not come because Jesus had not yet been "glorified." That could only come through His death, since the new covenant, like the old, was implemented by blood. Speaking to His disciples about His coming death He said:

"The hour has come for the Son of Man to be glorified." (John12:23)

The blood of the covenant

As the Lord and His disciples celebrated the Passover in the upper room, the Lord Jesus implemented a remembrance feast for them:

And he said to them, "I have eagerly desired to eat this Passover with you before I suffer. For I tell you, I will not eat of it again until it finds fulfilment in the kingdom of God." After taking the cup he gave thanks and said, "take this and divide it among you. For I tell you I will not drink again of the fruit of the vine until the kingdom of God comes." And he took bread, gave thanks and broke it, and gave it to them saying, "This is my body given for you: do this in remembrance of me." In the same way, after the supper he took the cup, saying, "This cup is the new covenant in my blood, which is poured out for you." (Luke 22:15-20)

A similar narrative is found in Matthew 26:26-29 and Mark 14:22-25, although in these passages most manuscripts use the term "covenant" rather than "new covenant."

There are a number of interesting points that emerge from this narrative:

- The occasion is the celebration of the Jewish Passover, the Israelites' remembrance of their deliverance from Egypt, when the blood of the lamb without blemish was splashed on the doorposts to protect them from death.
- Both the Passover and the ceremony the Lord was instituting were connected with the future coming of the kingdom of God.
- The disciples were told to eat the bread in remembrance of the Lord, presumably every time they celebrated Passover.
- The cup represented the new covenant in the Lord's blood. Here the Lord uses words similar to those spoken by Moses, when the old covenant was established – see footnote 2 on page 15 above.

The Acts church continued to celebrate this ceremony in obedience to the Lord's instructions to the disciples but Paul, writing to the Corinthians, sheds more light on the practice and how it was to be understood. Interestingly, Paul indicates that he received this from the Lord and not from a tradition handed down from the disciples.

> For I received from the Lord what I also passed on to you: The Lord Jesus, on the night he was betrayed took bread, and when he had given thanks, he broke it and said, "This is my body, which is for you; do this in remembrance of me." In the same way, after supper he took the cup saying, "This cup is the new covenant in my blood; do this, whenever you drink it, in remembrance of me." For whenever you eat this bread and drink this cup, you proclaim the Lord's death until he comes. (1 Corinthians 11:23-26)

In this passage, references to the coming of the kingdom of God have been replaced by a reference to the second coming of the Lord Jesus, presumably the same event. In addition, the celebration of this remembrance was a proclamation of the Lord's death.

So the great deliverer of the nation of Israel, foretold in the Old Testament, was the Lord Jesus. And He by His death would provide the blood for the sacrifice to enable the new covenant to be established. How was this to be?

To find the explanation of what was going on, we need to turn to the epistle to the Hebrews.

The new covenant in Hebrews

The first ten chapters of Hebrews explore the pre-eminence of the Lord Jesus Christ over all of the principal features of the Old Testament religious system of Israel.[5] One particular dimension of this is the superiority of the new covenant to the old covenant. There are three main ways in which the new covenant is better than the old.

1. It is supported by a better priesthood

Hebrews chapters 4-7 discuss the superiority of the Lord Jesus' priesthood in the order of Melchizedek, to the Aaronic priesthood. Hebrews 7:21 explains that:

> He became a priest with an oath when God said to him: "The Lord has sworn and will not change his mind: 'You

---

[5] For a more detailed discussion of this subject see *The Superiority of Christ*, by W M Henry.

are a priest forever.'" Because of this oath, Jesus has become the guarantee of a better covenant." (Hebrews 7:21-22)

The superiority of Christ's priesthood lies in the fact that, unlike the Aaronic priesthood, it was permanent (Hebrews 7:23-25). In addition, Christ, unlike the Aaronic priests, was pure and blameless (Hebrews 7:26-28) and therefore did not need to offer sacrifices for His own sin. Instead, He sacrificed for the people's sins once-for-all when He offered Himself as the sacrifice (Hebrews 7:27). Because of the permanent nature of Christ's priesthood confirmed by God's oath and the effectiveness of His once-for-all sacrifice, He became not only the *mediator* of a new covenant, but the *guarantee* that it will be fulfilled.

Hebrews 8-10 focus more closely on the superiority of Christ's sacrifice. He is now exalted above the heavens (Hebrews 7:26) and ministers as a priest in the true tabernacle, set up by the Lord (Hebrews 8:2), rather than the earthly tabernacle, where the Aaronic priests ministered.

2. It has a superior ministry because it is based on better promises.

We read of this in Hebrews 8:6:

> But the ministry Jesus has received is as superior to theirs as the covenant of which he is the mediator is superior to the old one, and it is founded on better promises. (Hebrews 8:6)

Why is it based on better promises? The problem was that the sacrificial system administered by the priests could only offer a figurative cleansing. It was not possible for the blood of bulls and goats to provide forgiveness of sins (Hebrews 10:4). However, the Lord Jesus' sacrifice of Himself enabled real cleansing from sin, and the permanent nature of His priesthood administered in the heavens guaranteed the people's continuing acceptance.

> For this reason Christ is the mediator of a new covenant, that those who are called may receive the promised eternal inheritance – now that he has died as a ransom to set them free from the sins committed under the first covenant. (Hebrews 9:15)

3. It is more effective because it is implemented by the work of the Holy Spirit

How were the people to be motivated to follow the Lord's ways? They had not been able to keep the old covenant, in spite of all their good intentions (see Exodus 19:8 and 24:3). Would the new covenant be any better? Hebrews 8:8-12 quotes Jeremiah's prophecy about the new covenant, which explains that the Lord will write His laws in their minds, by the work of the Spirit.

This is the basis on which the new covenant will succeed where the old one failed and Hebrews 10 summarises the arguments. The priesthood and sacrifices of the old covenant have been superseded by the priesthood and sacrifice of the Lord Jesus under the new. The Holy Spirit's work in the hearts of the people will be the key to their obedience:

> The Holy Spirit also testifies to us about this. First he says: "This is the covenant I will make with them *after that time*," says the Lord. I will put my laws in their hearts, and I will write them on their minds." Then he adds: "Their sins and their lawless acts I will remember no more." And where

these have been forgiven, there is no longer any sacrifice for sin. (Hebrews 10:15-18)

But when is this going to happen? It is to be "after that time." How does this relate to the work of the Holy Spirit at Pentecost and in the subsequent chapters in Acts?

Pentecost and afterwards

In Acts 1:3 we read that the risen Lord appeared to the disciples over a period of forty days and spoke to them about the kingdom of God. On one such occasion He gave them a specific instruction:

> Do not leave Jerusalem, but wait for the gift my Father promised, which you have heard me speak about. For John baptised with water, but in a few days you will be baptised with the Holy Spirit. (Acts 1:4-5)

The disciples' response to this is interesting.

> So, when they met together, they asked him, "Lord, are you at this time going to restore the kingdom to Israel?" (Acts 1:6)

We may be tempted to smile at the disciples' limited vision but it is reasonable to infer that such a question emerged logically from the Lord's forty days of instruction about the kingdom of God. It is also significant that Jesus' reply related only to the *timing* of that restoration, rather than to the *fact* of it.

> "It is not for you to know the times or dates the Father has set by his own authority." (Acts 1:7)

They were to receive the Holy Spirit's power so that they could be the Lord's witnesses, starting in Jerusalem but spreading out to the ends of the earth (verse 8).

This, of course, came about at Pentecost when the Holy Spirit came upon the disciples, as Joel had prophesied, in a way that had never been seen before. The context of Joel's prophecy was the restoration of Israel and from the Lord's words in Acts 1:7, this potentially could have been the time for the restoration of the kingdom. It would appear that Peter, when he stood up to address the crowd in Acts 2:14, anticipated that this would happen. In Acts 2:16 he declared that:

> "*This is* what was spoken by the prophet Joel: 'In the last days, God says, I will pour out my Spirit on all people[6]...'"

Peter's first sermon highlighted the fact the Christ was the heir of David:

> "He (David) was a prophet and knew that God had promised that he would place one of his descendants on his

---

[6] It has been pointed out that Joel and other Old Testament prophets suggest that the outpouring of the Spirit will take place *after* the kingdom has been established. See, for example *The Day of the Locust*, by Charles Ozanne, pp21-22, *The Burden of Prophecy* by Charles H Welch, p21 and *Joel's Prophecy: Past and Future* by Michael Penny, p54. Joel 2:28 says that the Spirit will be poured out "afterward" – i.e. after Israel has been restored. However, Peter, in Acts 2:17 amends this to "in the last days," and it does seem clear that he regarded what was happening at Pentecost as the *start* of the process that would lead to the restoration of the kingdom to Israel.

throne. Seeing what was ahead, he spoke of the resurrection of the Christ..." (Acts 2:30-31)

What the Jewish people had to do was

"Repent and be baptised, every one of you, in the name of Jesus Christ for the forgiveness of sins. And you will receive the gift of the Holy Spirit." (Acts 2:38)

Here Peter suggested that the indwelling of the Holy Spirit will be the first consequence of their repentance.

But the second consequence would be that the Lord would return and restore the kingdom to Israel, in fulfilment of Old Testament prophecy, as Peter says specifically in his second sermon.

"Repent, then, and turn to God, so that your sins may be wiped out, that times of refreshing may come from the Lord, and that he may send the Christ, who has been appointed for you – even Jesus. He must remain in heaven until the time comes for God to *restore everything* as he promised long ago through his holy prophets." (Acts 3:19-21)

As discussed on pages 8-13 above, the Lord's original promises to Abraham were unconditional and the climax of this sermon highlights the Lord's fulfilment of His covenant promises to Abraham's physical descendants.

"Indeed, all the prophets from Samuel on, as many as have spoken, have foretold these days. And you are the heirs of the prophets and the covenant God made with your fathers. He said to Abraham, 'Through your offspring all peoples on earth will be blessed.' When God raised up his servant, he sent him first to bless you by turning each of you from your wicked ways." (Acts 3:24-26)

The key markers for the implementation of the new covenant with Israel were being put into place:

- The guilt of the people had been taken away by the shedding of the blood of the new covenant and the establishment of an effectual priesthood in the order of Melchizedek.
- The ministry of the Lord Jesus, which was superior to the ministry of the old covenant because it was based on better promises, had been established.
- The risen, glorified Lord Jesus was identified as the rightful heir to David's throne.
- He was ready to return, if the people repented, to restore the kingdom to Israel.
- The critical feature of the new covenant, identified by Jeremiah and other prophets – the writing of the Lord's law in the hearts of the people by the Holy Spirit, had also begun to take place. Three thousand people were saved the first day (Acts 2:41) and the numbers continued to grow exponentially on a daily basis (Acts 2:47), reaching about five thousand by Acts 4:4.

The Law written on their hearts

Was the outpouring of the Spirit at Pentecost and afterwards the fulfilment of Joel's prophecy? Alternatively, was it a preliminary manifestation of a much greater outpouring that would take place in the future, after Christ's return?

It is clear from Peter's words in the early part of Acts that, as far as he was concerned, it was "all systems go" for the establishment of the kingdom and the implementation of the new covenant. In 2 Corinthians 3:6 Paul introduces himself and his companions as "ministers of a new covenant," and highlights the work of the Spirit:

> He has made us competent as ministers of a new covenant – not of the letter but of the Spirit. (2 Corinthians 3:6)

Earlier in the chapter, Paul spoke of the work of the Spirit in the hearts of the Corinthian believers in terms that are very reminiscent of those used in Jeremiah 31:33 in relation to the new covenant.

> You show that you are a letter from Christ, the result of our ministry, written not with ink but with the Spirit of the living God, not on human tablets of stone but on tablets of human hearts. (2 Corinthians 3:3)

The connection with the new covenant is picked up more strongly later in the same chapter, where Paul contrasts the superior glory of the ministry of the Spirit with the inferior glory of the ministry of the old covenant.

> Now if the ministry that brought death, which was engraved in letters on stone, came with glory ... will not the ministry of the Spirit be even more glorious? If the ministry that condemns men is glorious, how much more glorious is the ministry that brings righteousness ... Therefore, since we have such a hope, we are very bold. We are not like Moses, who would put a veil over his face to keep the Israelites from gazing at it while the radiance was fading away. But their minds were made dull, for to this day the same veil remains when the old covenant is read. It has not been removed, because only in Christ is it taken away ... But whenever anyone turns to the Lord, the veil is taken away. Now the Lord is the Spirit, and where the Spirit of the Lord is, there is freedom. And we, who with unveiled faces all reflect the Lord's glory, are being transformed into his

likeness with ever-increasing glory, which comes from the Lord, who is the Spirit. (2 Corinthians 3:7-18)

What a wonderful description of the transforming power of the Holy Spirit on the hearts of the Lord's people! Surely this was what Joel and Jeremiah were anticipating for the whole nation of Israel?

Yet, as we compare these events with the prophets' vision, we see that they anticipated something even more wide-ranging than the events in Acts – the entire nation of Israel indwelt by the Spirit. This was not happening. Even by Acts 4, opposition was growing. Peter and John were arrested, threatened and warned not to speak any more in the name of Jesus. That opposition grew to open persecution as Acts progressed.

Also, the constitution of the church was changing. In the early days, only Jews were becoming Christians. Peter, though he acknowledged that blessing would flow to all peoples on earth (Acts 3:26), evidently thought that this would only happen after the Lord returned, the kingdom was established, and Israel as a nation of priests would minister to all other nations. It took a vision, instruction from the Holy Spirit and a visit to Cornelius to broaden his perspective. When the Lord appeared to Saul on the Damascus road, He commissioned him to take the Gospel to Gentiles as well as to the people of Israel (Acts 9:15; see also 22:21).

What was happening? And how does this affect the implementation of the new covenant? The implications of these developments will be considered in the final chapter.

The Place of the Gentiles

The Place of the Gentiles

The new covenant revisited

The covenants with Abraham, Moses and David all found their consummation in the new covenant. This new covenant had a number of features:

- The covenant was ratified by the shedding of the blood of the Lord Jesus Christ, poured out as a perfect sacrifice for sins, in contrast with the ineffective sacrifices of the Mosaic covenant.
- The Lord Jesus has now been established as priest over the new order, in a permanent priesthood operating in the real tabernacle in heaven, in contrast to the earthly priesthood and tabernacle of the Mosaic covenant.
- The two houses of Israel will be re-united as promised by Jeremiah.
- The nation will return to the land as promised in the Abrahamic covenant.
- The monarchy will be restored with the Lord Jesus as king of Israel in David's line as promised in the Davidic covenant.
- God's laws would be written on the hearts of the people by the power of the Holy Spirit as promised by Jeremiah and in contrast to the ineffective operation of the Mosaic covenant.

Peter and the rest of the disciples at Pentecost and after, sought, under the Spirit's power, to proclaim the message that Jesus was Israel's Messiah. When individuals repented, the Holy Spirit came upon them as the prophets had predicted. But there was not a complete repentance of the nation. The Jewish leaders in particular would not accept the message and began to oppose the work of the apostles. So what was to happen?

In addition, as Acts progressed, a further change took place – Gentiles began to come to faith and were included in the Acts church.

The inclusion of Gentiles in Acts

In Acts 9 we read of the conversion of Saul, the great persecutor of the fledgling church. He, like Peter, initially focused on Jews. His vast knowledge of the Jewish scriptures enabled him to offer Scriptural proof that Jesus was the Messiah (the Christ).

> Saul grew more and more powerful and baffled the Jews living in Damascus by proving that Jesus is the Christ. (Acts 9:22)

But in Acts 10, Peter received a vision and was directed to preach to Cornelius. As he spoke to him and his friends, the Holy Spirit came on these Gentiles, to the amazement of Peter and his colleagues:

> The circumcised believers who had come with Peter were astonished that the gift of the Holy Spirit had been poured out even on the Gentiles. (Acts 10:45)

Yet this was not entirely unexpected. Isaiah had said long before that:

> Foreigners who bind themselves to the Lord to serve him, to love the name of the Lord, and to worship him, all who keep the Sabbath without desecrating it and who hold fast to my covenant – these I will bring to my holy mountain

and give them joy in the house of prayer. Their burnt offerings and sacrifices will be accepted on my altar; for my house will be called a house of prayer for all nations. (Isaiah 56:6-8)

So, there is a precedent for Gentiles to be included in Israel's covenant blessings. And as individual Gentiles believed the Gospel, they were included within the growing church. But what was their relationship with the Jewish believers? Paul explains what was happening in Romans 11, in his picture of Israel as an olive tree. He describes the "natural" branches of the Jewish olive tree being broken off and "wild" olive branches (Gentiles) being grafted in to "share in the nourishing sap from the olive root" (verse 17). The purpose of this was to stimulate the olive tree (Israel) to make it respond. Or, in plain words:

> Because of their transgression, salvation has come to the Gentiles *to make Israel envious* ... in the hope that I may somehow arouse my own people to envy and save some of them. (Romans 11:11, 14)

Gentiles, then, were being included in Israel's blessings, obtaining the "nourishing sap" from the Jewish tree. The hope was that unrepentant Israel would return to the Lord. Paul sums it up plainly at the end of the section.

> Israel has experienced a hardening in part until the full number of the Gentiles has come in. And so all Israel will be saved, as it is written: "The deliverer will come from Zion; he will turn ungodliness away from Jacob. And this is my covenant with them when I take away their sins." (Romans 11:25-27)

So is this a fair description of what has happened over the last 2,000 years? Is the full number of Gentile believers still "coming in" to something that is essentially Israel's? And is God still anticipating that Israel will repent?

Acts 28 and after

The facts are that the Holy Spirit was not poured out on the whole nation of Israel and, arguably more critically, the Lord did not return to set up His kingdom at that time. So what happened? Were Peter and the rest of the disciples mistaken in expecting this, or did changing circumstances cause a postponement of the restoration of the kingdom to Israel?

The Lord in Acts 1:7 had indicated that the timing was uncertain, at least as far as the disciples were concerned.

Perhaps the interpretation of Joel's prophecy that places the complete outpouring of the Spirit on the nation after Christ's return and the restoration of the kingdom is correct (see footnote on page 48). Zechariah describes the return of Christ to the Mount of Olives to deliver Israel from her enemies:

> And I will pour out on the house of David and the inhabitants of Jerusalem a spirit of grace and supplication. They will look on me, the one they have pierced, and they will mourn for him as one mourns for an only child. (Zechariah 12:10)

Zechariah's picture is one of a nation shocked and horrified at the identity of their deliverer – the Lord Jesus, the One they had pierced and for generations have rejected.

The inclusion of Gentiles in Israel's blessings during the period covered by the Acts of the Apostles was not incompatible with the implementation of the new covenant and the establishment of the kingdom. Throughout Acts, however, although the message was being taken to Gentiles, the apostles tended to seek out Jews first and proclaim the Gospel to them, before turning to Gentiles when the Jewish people did not repent. For example, in Acts 13:5, we find Barnabas and Saul sent to Cyprus, where they proclaimed the word of God in the Jewish synagogues; similarly in Pisidian Antioch in Acts 13:14. When the Jews there talked abusively against Paul and Barnabas, they turned to the Gentiles. Paul, significantly comments:

> We had to speak the word of God to you first. Since you reject it and do not consider yourselves worthy of eternal life, we now turn to the Gentiles. (Acts 13:46; see also Romans 1:16, which was written during the Acts period.)

When Paul finally arrived as a prisoner in Rome in Acts 28, he called the Jewish leaders together three days after arriving there (verse 17), told them that he was a prisoner "because of the hope of Israel" (verse 20) and subsequently engaged them in discussion about Jesus from the Law of Moses and the Prophets (verse 23).

When they could not agree among themselves, Paul quoted Isaiah 6:9,10 to them[7] and made this final pronouncement:

> "The Holy Spirit spoke the truth to your forefathers when he said through Isaiah the Prophet: 'Go to this people and say, "You will be ever hearing but never understanding; you will be ever seeing but never perceiving." For this people's heart has become calloused; they hardly hear with

---

[7] For a discussion of the significance of this passage see *The Most Quoted Old Testament Prophecy* by Michael Penny, published by The Open Bible Trust.

their ears, and have closed their eyes. Otherwise they might see with their eyes, hear with their ears, understand with their hearts and turn and I would heal them.' Therefore I want you to know that God's salvation has been sent to the Gentiles and they will listen!" (Acts 28:25-28)

This is the final time in the New Testament that Isaiah 6 is quoted. This is significant and was obviously something more than a comment on the local situation, such as Paul had made in Acts 13. The Jewish leaders continued to reject Jesus and, within a few years, the Jerusalem temple was destroyed by the Romans and Israel ceased to exist as a nation. From then on, the leadership of the first century churches increasingly became dominated by Gentiles.

However, more importantly, when we read Paul's epistles written after Acts 28 (Ephesians, Philippians, Colossians, Philemon, 1 and 2 Timothy and Titus), we find only one reference to the covenants (in Ephesians 2:12, where Paul describes the past condition of Gentiles as being "foreigners to the covenants of the promise."). In these later epistles there are no references to Abraham, Isaac or Jacob, only one reference to David (2 Timothy 2:8) and a single reference to Moses (2 Timothy 3:8).

Instead, in Ephesians and Colossians we find Paul's revelation of a secret or "mystery" which had not been revealed in previous generations. This concerns a group of believers described as "his body" in Colossians 1:24. Paul states that:

> I have become its (the church's) servant by the commission God gave me to present to you the word of God in its fullness – the mystery that has been kept hidden for ages and generations, but is now disclosed to the saints. To them God has chosen to make known among the Gentiles the

glorious riches of this mystery, which is Christ in you, the hope of glory. (Colossians 1:25-27)

This mystery is Christ in you Gentiles, the hope of glory. The same point is made in Ephesians.

In Ephesians 3, Paul describes himself as the prisoner of Christ Jesus for you Gentiles. This is in contrast to what he said to the Jews in Acts 28:20:

> "It is because of the hope of Israel that I am bound with this chain."

Instead, he declares that he has received a revelation of a mystery (verse 3). He goes on:

> In reading this, then, you will be able to understand my insight into the mystery of Christ, which was not made known to men in other generations as it has now been revealed by the Spirit to God's holy apostles and prophets. This mystery is that through the gospel the Gentiles are heirs together with Israel, members together of one body, and sharers together in the promise in Christ Jesus. (Ephesians 3:4-6)

It is unfortunate that the NIV translation includes the words "with Israel" as these are not in the original. The point is that individual Gentiles and individual Jews are joint members of a joint body and joint sharers in the promise in Christ, through the Gospel. This is something very different from what happened during Acts when individual Gentile believers were being brought into a group that was essentially a redeemed Israel. It is also highly significant that Paul states in both Colossians and Ephesians that this truth had not previously been revealed, a point he repeats again in Ephesians 3:9

where he speaks of the mystery "which for ages past was kept hidden in God, who created all things."

The fact that Gentiles were to be blessed was no hidden mystery; nor was the new covenant and the attendant blessings extended to Gentiles. These had been revealed earlier in both the Old and New Testaments. Here, for the first time, we have a joint body with Jewish and Gentile believers having equal status and with Christ as the Head of the body.

However, it is important to realise that the foundational truths of the Gospel remain the same. God's household is:

> built on the foundation of the apostles and prophets, with Christ Jesus as the chief cornerstone. (Ephesians 2:20)

The great Scriptural doctrines like justification by faith hammered out in Romans still stand; the Holy Spirit indwells *all* believers and develops His fruit in our lives, conforming us to the image of our Lord and Head, Jesus Christ. Hence, Scriptures written to believers in different circumstances to our own are still relevant to us. As Paul in his final epistle says to Timothy:

> *All Scripture* is God-breathed and is useful for teaching, rebuking, correcting and training in righteousness, so that the man of God may be thoroughly equipped for every good work. (2 Timothy 3:16-17)

What of the future?

As we consider the Lord's statements concerning the ultimate fulfilment of His promises to His ancient people, Israel, it is hard to escape the conclusion that He intends one day to implement them. Israel as a nation may not be at the heart of His purposes at the present time, but at the appropriate "time or date" (Acts 1:7), He will resume His purposes for Israel, redeeming them, pouring out His Spirit into their hearts and making them a blessing to the peoples of the earth.

More on Covenants

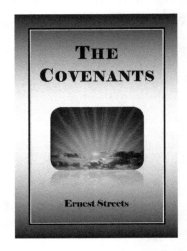

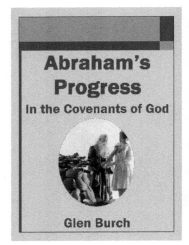

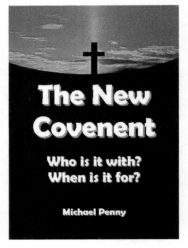

Please visit **www.obt.org.uk** for further details of these books.

These books can be ordered from that website.

They are also available as eBooks from Amazon and Apple and as KDP paperbacks from Amazon..

Index of Books Referred to

Burch, Glen, *Abraham's Progress in the Covenants of God*, The Open Bible Trust

Henry, W M, *The Superiority of Christ*, The Open Bible Trust

Ozanne, Charles, *The Day of the Locust*, The Open Bible Trust

Penny, Michael, *Joel's Prophecy: Past and Future,* The Open Bible Trust

Penny, Michael, *Prophets, Kings & Chronicles*, Berean Publishing Trust

Penny, Michael, *The Most Quoted Old Testament Prophecy*, The Open Bible Trust

Streets, Ernest, *Think on These Things*, The Open Bible Trust

Welch, Charles H, *The Burden of Prophecy*, Berean Publishing Trust

About the author

W. M. Henry was born in Glasgow in 1949. He qualified as a Chartered Accountant and worked in the accountancy profession for a number of years before moving into academia. At present he is working as an  education consultant. He lives in Giffnock with his wife and two daughters.

Other books by W M Henry include:

The Trinity in John
No Condemnation – Romans 5:12-8:39
That you may know – 1 John
The Speeches in Acts
The Making of a Man of God
The Superiority of Christ

The Signs in John's Gospel
Living in the Truth
The Greatness of Christ
By Faith Abraham
Imitating Christ

He has also written four books with Michael Penny

Following Philippians
The Will of God: Past and Present
Who is Jesus?
Sit! Walk! Stand! The Christian Life in Ephesians

Please visit **www.obt.org.uk** for further details. These books can be ordered from that website.

They are also available as eBooks from Amazon and Apple and as KDP paperbacks from Amazon..

W M Henry is a regular contributor to *Search* magazine

For a free sample of
The Open Bible Trust's magazine *Search*,
please visit

www.obt.org.uk/search

or email

admin@obt.org.uk

Further Reading

The Will of God: Past and Present

W M Henry and Michael Penny

It is imperative in the study of any subject to consider *all* that the Bible has to say.

This book does just that: starting in Genesis it works its way through the Bible chronologically.

It pays attention to when new aspects of the will of God are revealed, and to why these changes occur.

In the New Testament, the authors have taken special care to distinguish between the will of God for Jews and His will for Gentiles. Sometimes it is the same … but not always.

****

Please visit **www.obt.org.uk** for further details of this book and the ones on the next pages.

These books can be ordered from that website.

They are also available as eBooks from Amazon and Apple and as KDP paperbacks from Amazon..

Following Philippians

W M Henry & Michael Penny

This book from William Henry and Michael Penny is much more than a commentary. It is a verse by verse exploration and discussion.

The authors first examine what a passage would have meant to the original first century Philippians, before seeking applications for 21st century Christians.

Each chapter of the book deals with a particular passage in Philippians in a number of ways.

- First, the Big Issues set out the main points of the passage
- Then the passage is Explored with helpful insights into the historical setting of first century Philippi and the issues of that day
- This is followed by a set of Comprehension Questions on the passage
- Next, the passage is Discussed in a manner which takes what has been learnt and discusses it, using it to direct light onto today's Christian experiences
- Each chapter concludes with a set of Contemplation Questions on the passage.

The result is a study guide to Philippians which balances well-researched historical information with practical lessons for today's Christian.

Think on These Things

Ernest Streets

This book deals with a number of well-known subjects, but Ernest Streets has some distinctive and different insights which readers will find both interesting and helpful, as well as thought-provoking. The table of contents is as follows:

- Think on these things
    - Paul's Ministry
    - The Gospel of your salvation (Ephesians 1:13)
    - The Eternal Purpose in Christ Jesus our Lord (Ephesians 3:11)
    - The Mystery of the Gospel (Ephesians 6:19)
    - The Body of Christ (Ephesians 4:12)
- Do you understand what you are reading?
- These signs ... Mark 16:17
    - To the Jew first
    - Scriptural proof of the "living hope"
    - The last twelve verses of Mark's Gospel
- The Covenants
- The Lord's Table
- Another Look at the Gospel of John

■■

**A full list of publications by
The Open Bible Trust can be seen at
www.obt.org.uk**

About this book

Covenants: Old and New

The introduction deals with covenants in general, explaining the meaning and purpose of covenants in the Bible and how they were ratified.

We are then given the details of three important covenants; the ones God made with ... Abraham ... the Nation of Israel at Sinai ... and David. Next follows a brief history of the Nation after Solomon before dealing with the New Covenant in the rest of the Old Testament.

This is followed by a consideration of the New Covenant in the New Testament, and the final chapter deals with the place of Gentiles with respect to covenants.

www.ingramcontent.com/pod-product-compliance
Lightning Source LLC
LaVergne TN
LVHW012157010625
812740LV00009B/728